It's CHRISTMAS!

ALL ABOUT THE
NORTH POLE

KRISTEN RAJCZAK NELSON

PowerKiDS
press™

NEW YORK

Published in 2020 by The Rosen Publishing Group, Inc.
29 East 21st Street, New York, NY 10010

First Edition

Editor: Kristen Nelson
Book Design: Reann Nye

Photo Credits: Cover Aleksei Verhovski/Shutterstock.com; p. 5 wavebreakmedia/Shutterstock.com; p. 7 Istimages/Shutterstock.com; p. 9 jorisvo/Shutterstock.com; p.11 Vladimir Melnikov/Shutterstock.com; p. 13 Bettmann/Getty Images; p. 15 https://commons. wikimedia.org/wiki/File:Santa_Claus_1863_Harpers.png; p. 17 Transcendental Graphics/Getty Images; p. 19 Kit Leong/ Shutterstock.com; p. 21 Roman Babakin/Shutterstock.com; p. 22 Peter Dench/Getty Images.

Library of Congress Cataloging-in-Publication Data

Names: Rajczak Nelson, Kristen, author.
Title: All about the North Pole / Kristen Rajczak Nelson.
Description: New York : PowerKids Press [2020] | Series: It's Christmas! | Includes webography. | Includes index.
Identifiers: LCCN 2018046623| ISBN 9781725300880 (paperback) | ISBN
  9781725300903 (library bound) | ISBN 9781725300897 (6 pack)
Subjects: LCSH: North Pole–Juvenile literature.
Classification: LCC G635 .R28 2020 | DDC 394.2663–dc23
LC record available at https://lccn.loc.gov/2018046623

CPSIA Compliance Information: Batch #CSPK19. For Further Information contact Rosen Publishing, New York, New York at 1-800-237-9932.

CONTENTS

SANTA AT HOME

Most stories of Santa Claus start at his home and workshop at the North Pole. That's where he checks his list of children who have been **naughty** and nice. His reindeer and the elves are pictured living there, too! But why do we believe Santa lives so far north?

THE TOP OF THE WORLD

The North Pole is a real place! It's found in the Arctic Ocean and isn't on a piece of land. It's the northernmost end of a line that goes through the center of Earth. This line is called Earth's axis. The planet turns around this axis. Could Santa—or anyone—live there?

MAN FROM MYRA

The story of Santa comes from the true story of a man named Nicholas. He lived between AD 270 and 343. Now known as Saint Nicholas of Myra, he lived quite far from the Arctic Ocean and the North Pole. He lived in what is present-day Turkey in the Middle East! Over time, though, his story grew.

9

GETTING COLDER

By the 1800s, Saint Nicholas was called Santa Claus in many places. Then, a poem called "A Visit from Saint Nicholas" came out in 1823. It said that Santa traveled with "eight tiny reindeer." Reindeer are found in cold places. So, Santa began to be **associated** with the ice and snow found where reindeer live.

11

NAST'S PICTURES

The location of Santa's home and workshop became more **specific** because of an artist named Thomas Nast. Nast was a **political** cartoonist. His work was on the cover of and in magazines in both the United States and England during the late 1800s. Nast's cartoons made him famous.

13

Starting during the 1860s, Nast drew **illustrations** at Christmastime. These pictures often featured Santa. Before this, Santa's story didn't include any specific home. Some of Nast's pictures placed Santa at the North Pole! These works also shaped how Santa is pictured today—with a long white beard, round belly, and twinkle in his eye.

WHY THERE?

During the mid- to late 1800s, **explorers** were trying to reach the North Pole. The public closely followed the stories about these **expeditions**, but no one would reach it until 1908 or 1909. When Nast was drawing Santa living there, the North Pole was still a very **mysterious** place.

A Merry Christmas.

17

THE REAL NORTH POLES

Whether or not Santa Claus could live and work at the **geographic** North Pole, many people imagine that he does! Some have even founded places to visit based around the North Pole. Both North Pole, New York, and North Pole, Alaska, have been home to Santa's workshop or house!

19

There's another place closer to the geographic North Pole where Santa is said to live. The people of Rovaniemi, Finland, began building Santa's Village in 1950. It started because First Lady Eleanor Roosevelt was visiting and said she wanted to see Santa Claus. Today, visitors can see Santa 365 days a year!

NORTH POLE MAIL

Santa's hometown might not be exactly at the geographic North Pole. But if you send him a letter at Christmastime, that's still where you'll address the letter. If you send it through U.S. mail, you might even get a letter back—from the North Pole!

GLOSSARY

associated: Related to or connected with something else.

expedition: A journey for a certain purpose.

explorer: One who travels to a place to learn about it.

geographic: Having to do with or belonging to a certain area.

illustration: A picture or drawing in a publication.

mysterious: Strange or unknown.

naughty: Having to do with acting badly.

political: Having to do with government.

specific: Having to do with a certain person, thing, or situation.

INDEX

WEBSITES

Due to the changing nature of Internet links, PowerKids Press has developed an online list of websites related to the subject of this book. This site is updated regularly. Please use this link to access the list: www.powerkidslinks.com/IC/northpole